Don't Let the System Beat You

Don't Let the System Beat You

Dwayne Wallace

LexxiKhan Presents Publishing

LexxiKhan Presents Publishing
www.LexxiKhanPresents.com

Ordering information:
Quantity sales. Special discounts are available on quantity purchases by corporations, associations, and others. For details, contact the publisher at the web address above.

This book is dedicated to every child in the foster care system. You and your story matter. Keep going. You've got this.

CONTENTS

DEDICATION   v
FOREWORD   ix
MY GIFT TO YOU   xi

Introduction

1 | Lesson One: Get a Plan   4

2 | Lesson 2: Use Short-Term Goals to Help with Your Plan   14

3 | Lesson Three: Lock In   23

4 | Lesson Four: Use Your Gifts & Talents to Your Advantage   35

5 | Lesson Five: Get a Mentor   42

6 | Lesson Six: Be a Good Mentee   48

7 | Lesson Seven: Get Serious About Your Financial Future   55

8 | Lesson Eight: Build Your Resume Now   60

9 | Lesson Nine: Watch the Company You Keep   64

CONTENTS

10 | Lesson Ten: Build a Solid Support
System   66

11 | Lesson Eleven: Constantly Work to
Improve Your Relationship with Your Mentor   69

A Message from Glae

A Message From My Mentor Tammy

A Message From My Mentor Gabby

A Message From Coach Kevin

A Message From My Program Director
David

12 | Lesson Twelve: Never Give Up   87

13 | Lesson Thirteen: Maintain an Attitude
of Gratitude   93

JOIN OUR BOOK CLUB   99

By Dr. Allanah Roberts-Headley

Hello, I'm Dr. Allanah Roberts-Headley. Prior to becoming a mental health counselor and a Doctor of Education, I first started my career as a case manager for the foster care system in the state of Florida. At first, I only took the job because it was the only opportunity I had post-undergrad with a psychology degree, but after my first year in this position, I knew that I had a passion for helping children who were victims of the system. I continued as a case manager for six years within the foster care system with a huge focus on transitional-age youth over the age of thirteen before becoming a mental health counselor that served the foster care population, which I am actively still providing services to.

My personal and professional experiences are why I feel like Dwayne Wallace's book *Don't Let the System Beat You* is a vital read for young adults presently navigating the foster care system. In these pages, you'll find real-life stories, practical advice, and the tools to help you discover your inner strength. No matter where you are on your journey, whether you're still in school or taking your first steps into the world on your own, this book is for you. It's a roadmap to help you overcome obstacles and reach for your dreams, starting right now.

Dwayne Wallace's personal experiences and hard-won lessons are shared in a way that's easy to understand and apply. It's not just about surviving; it's about thriving and taking charge of your future. You have a ton of untapped potential within you, and this book can help you unlock it.

It's important to remember that your past doesn't define you. No matter where you come from or what obstacles are in front of you, you have the power to shape your future. So, let's embark on this journey together. Read, learn, and take action. Use this book as a tool to craft the life you want. Your future is waiting, and you have the strength to create it. The path may not always be easy, but with the wisdom in these pages, you can face any challenge and build the future you envision. There is no other moment to wait for. **Reinvent yourself - right now.**

Before we begin, I want to encourage you to download your FREE copy of my guided journal. Make sure you get an adult's permission first. Then, I want you to head over to LexxiKhanPresents.com/dwayne and download your FREE journal. You will need this as a companion to this book because I will challenge you to write out your plans and journal your thoughts. Together, my hope is that you develop a habit of self-reflecting, journaling, and using strategies to help you get ahead.

If you have any issues obtaining your free copy of my guided journal, please have an adult send an email to: **wecare@lexxikhanpresents.com**

Introduction

If you're reading these words, know that you're not alone in your current situation. In the United States, there are over 400,000 children in foster care, and perhaps you're one of them. I've been where you are, faced similar challenges, and navigated through tough times. This book is my humble attempt to share what I've learned along the way so I can encourage you on your journey.

I created this book *Don't Let the System Beat You* to be a guide designed exclusively for young adults like you who are currently navigating the trenches of the foster care system. Because I didn't always follow the advice I'm about to share with you, my journey was sometimes harder than it needed to be; however, luckily for me, I had people in my corner who wouldn't allow me to quit, and I hope to be one of those people for you.

My name is Dwayne Wallace, and I'm not your typical author. In fact, if you knew how much I struggled with writing and grammar growing up, you would be surprised that I even wrote a book. Even with that being true, I graduated from one of the top colleges in the world and completed things that most people dream about. Let that be proof that your current situations don't define you or your outcomes.

Before we begin, I want to emphasize the significance of the following thirteen chapters. Sometimes, they may seem repetitive. I've done that with intention. Each chapter will stress the importance of creating a plan, sticking to it, and overcoming every opponent trying to knock you off your course.

My path here wasn't an easy one. I've faced more rejections than I want to name. I've had to deal with countless struggles, from navigating the complexities of going to school in three different countries to having to complete 60 credits in only three semesters so I wouldn't end up homeless. At times, I found myself feeling upset or hopeless about my situation. I also had seasons where I didn't show up as my best self, which impacted my ability to play football. That meant that I was unable to step onto a football field. The place that felt like my sanctuary during my most difficult times.

Despite every challenge I've ever encountered, I've clung to a plan and an attitude of gratitude. Even in my darkest hours, I knew I was not a victim and had full control over my life and future. I refused to let anything define me or dictate the course of my life. Instead, I channeled all my energy into the things I had control over. No matter what, I had control over my mind and my will to learn new skills.

This book is not about dwelling on the past or *playing the victim*. No, my friend, it's about harnessing the power within you, discovering your strengths, and forging your own path to a brighter future than you can imagine. It's about flipping the script and showing yourself and the world what you're made of.

Before we begin, I want to set some expectations with you. There will be times when my advice might come off as harsh or challenging. That is because there may be times when the information I'm giving can't be watered down or presented in a nicer way. Either way, I want you to understand that it is all love from my side. I hope to be, for you, what I needed when I was sitting where you are today.

Finally, throughout this book, you will see a lot of football references. That's because football helped me during my difficult seasons. I encourage you to find another way to translate all of this information into an easy way for you to apply it.

So, are you ready to take control of your destiny? Are you prepared to embrace the challenges, defy the odds, and build a life that surpasses even your wildest dreams? If you answered "yes," buckle up, my friend. Together, we will shatter expectations, rise above limitations, and prove that we are unstoppable.

Let's dive in and discover the thirteen transformative lessons that will empower you to rise, thrive, and rewrite your own story.

> **Disclaimer**: Before we begin, I want to make something clear. I'm sharing *my* experience. In California, where I grew up, the transition program I was a part of provided housing until my 21st birthday. Don't assume your program is the same. Make sure you check the details with your case worker.

1

Lesson One: Get a Plan

Imagine this: your 21st birthday is quickly approaching. While those around you are eagerly planning a night of fun and bliss, you're stuck trying to piece your life together before everything fumbles at your fingertips. This can - and will - happen if you don't properly train for that day now.

As a former foster child, I understand the weight that rests on your shoulders every day. I know you don't always have the energy to do what needs to be done. Trust me, I understand. I'm not going to lie to you. The road ahead is going to be scary since things are a little uncertain right now. But I want you to know that you have the power to not only navigate this time and season of your life but also to end up a winner at the end of it all.

Again, I want to remind you that the age of emancipation is going to change depending on where you are. For some, it may be 18, for others, 21, and in certain cases, it could even be older. Regardless of age, one thing is going to remain the same in each situation. You have to speak up for yourself and be your best advocate. The more you know - the more you can protect your rights and make informed decisions.

While I personally used a lot of the tips that I'm going to share within this book, there were moments where I missed my mark, too. Those who know me know that I am someone who is quick to remind others that I make mistakes, too. Throughout this journey together, I don't expect perfection, and neither should you. As you grow older, you'll one day learn that it's through our mistakes and setbacks that we learn, grow, and become stronger.

To kick us off, I titled this chapter "Get a Plan" so we can lay a solid foundation for your success. Navigating the foster care system as you transition into adulthood is not a simple thing to do, but having a plan will make it easier. Just like a player would prepare for a football game, success requires careful planning, strategic thinking, and relentless execution.

66   NAVIGATING THE FOSTER CARE SYSTEM AS YOU TRANSITION   99
INTO ADULTHOOD IS NOT A SIMPLE THING TO DO, BUT HAVING
A PLAN WILL MAKE IT EASIER.

Assessing the field

Just like a skilled quarterback has to scan the defense before he makes a play, it's imperative that you assess the field in your own life. Right now, you have tools, programs, and people around you that can help you reach your goals. While your opponent, or the obstacles you face along the way, are going to change, you have to create a plan - something that will drive you forward.

In this section, we are going to discover the importance of strategic planning. I decided to start the book off like this because I still use it in my everyday life. I like doing everything with a clear and concise plan. It minimizes the room you have to make a mistake, and it makes it easier for other people to help you when they can understand your vision.

On the flip side, assessing the field is not just about preparing for obstacles and challenges. It's also about recognizing the unique strengths and abilities you possess that make you unstoppable. Whether you recognize it or not, you have the ability to transform the challenges you face today into lessons that will one day change someone else. The resilience and the determination that you are building now will be the fuel you need to push you further than you could have ever imagined.

During this time, I really want you to take an inventory of the goals you want to accomplish, and don't be afraid to think big. For me, I always knew that I wanted to make it to the big leagues. I wanted to suit up with my favorite players and play the sport I love at a professional level. That is why every decision I made was in pursuit of that goal. I also want you to have an open mind so you can consider all of the obstacles that may show up as you are chasing down those goals. By carefully evaluating the field, you will have a clearer understanding of your aspirations, your capabilities, and the potential opponents that you'll face along the way. This knowledge is going to be the key to having a solid foundation for your game plan.

For now, I want you to rise above every noise and distraction that is fighting for your time and attention. Instead, I want you to think about what truly matters - your dreams, your future, and your potential for greatness. So, metaphorically speaking, grab your helmet, and let's take that first step to victory.

> " I WANT YOU TO RISE ABOVE EVERY NOISE AND DISTRACTION " THAT IS FIGHTING FOR YOUR TIME AND ATTENTION. INSTEAD, I WANT YOU TO THINK ABOUT WHAT TRULY MATTERS - YOUR DREAMS, YOUR FUTURE, AND YOUR POTENTIAL FOR GREATNESS.

Scouting Your Goals

In football, scouts are used to locate the best of the best to help move an organization forward. For a minute, I want you to be a scout for your gifts and talents. Just like a skilled scout identifies talented players, it's time for you to recognize your own unique abilities that can propel you to success. What are some things that you can do to help move you and your career forward?

Think about the tools you currently possess, whether it's your creativity, intelligence, perseverance, or any other special qualities. These are your gifts, and they hold the key to unlocking opportunities. Just as I used my size and quick thinking to my advantage, it's crucial for you to identify your own strengths and determine how you can use them to create a pathway to your dreams.

But what exactly is a goal? A **goal** is more than just a wish. It's a clear and specific target that you set for yourself. It is something that you have to work to achieve. Goals help you by providing direction and purpose. They help you stay focused and motivated for something bigger than you can achieve right now.

When you are setting goals, it is important to consider both **short-term** and **long-term** objectives. Short-term goals are the small steps that lead you to the long-term vision. They are usually small goals that you can achieve within one to three months to help you with the bigger picture. A long-term goal, on the other hand, is the final destination that you are working towards.

To help you understand this, let's use another football reference. In football, scoring touchdowns is the ultimate goal, but it takes a series of strategic plays to get there. Getting the touchdown is your long-term goal. Having a successful play during your four attempts to move the ball ten yards is your short-term goal.

Similarly, in your life, you will have a long-term goal that you need to work towards. In order to get there, you are going to have smaller goals to help you get there.

Just as football teams strategize and execute plays to reach the end zone, you too have to design a game plan that incorporates both short-term and long-term goals. Each short-term goal brings you closer to the long-term victory, just like each successful play brings the team closer to scoring a touchdown.

By setting clear, actionable short-term goals and aligning them with your long-term vision, you will create a winning game plan for your life. Now, I want you to take a moment and develop your own game plan.

Keep your eyes focused on your end zone and don't lose site of your bigger picture.

> " A **GOAL** IS MORE THAN JUST A WISH. IT'S A CLEAR AND SPE- "
> CIFIC TARGET THAT YOU SET FOR YOURSELF. IT IS SOMETHING
> THAT YOU HAVE TO WORK TO ACHIEVE. GOALS HELP YOU BY
> PROVIDING DIRECTION AND PURPOSE.

Defining Your End Zone

Success is different for everyone. When I first started playing football, I thought success was defined by the amount of money in my wallet. Over time, I quickly learned that I didn't have to define success the same as everyone else. Now, as I grow older, success for me is about helping those around me and having the freedom to enjoy my life however I want to.

When I was still planning out my young adult life, my 'end zone' consisted of me playing for the National Football League. I knew that in order to reach my goals, I needed to continue to get as much playing time as I could. That's why graduating and receiving scholarships became my immediate short-term goals to help me reach my end zone.

Setting goals is imperative in mapping out your path to success. They provide structure, direction, and a sense of purpose. So, I want to challenge you to consider what your goals are. What is it that you want to achieve when you emancipate from your current program? What actions can you take to bring yourself closer to that goal?

Think about specific accomplishments you want to attain. Do you aspire to further your education, secure stable employment, build strong relationships, or develop a particular skill? Visualize your desired outcome and then break down the steps that you need to take in order to get it done. By setting clear and measurable goals, you create a roadmap that leads you toward your dreams.

Also, I want to point out that your goals are not set in stone. They can evolve and change as you progress and discover new opportunities available to you. No matter where your goals take you, embrace the journey of self-discovery and remain adaptable to all new chances that come your way. With a defined long-term goal and the plans to get there, you will be well-equipped to navigate and score touchdowns in the pursuit of your success.

Analyzing Your Skillset: Leveraging Your Unique Talents

Just like a football team thrives on the diverse skills and abilities of its players, you possess a set of unique talents that can propel you towards success. To help you with this part, I've briefly listed a few skills and how they can be beneficial to someone who is willing to acknowledge them as strengths. Can you think of any other ones that I might have missed?

- **Communication Skills**: Maybe you are able to tell a story like no one else. These skills transfer over to countless fields. From advocating for yourself to collaborating with others, by building your communication skills, you can strengthen a skill that is in high demand.
- **Problem-Solving Skills**: It is truly an art to analyze a problem and then find a creative solution for it. These skills can be used in jobs that require you to solve problems.
- **Creativity**: Thinking outside of the box can really pay off in the long run. This skill can be channeled into art, entrepreneurship, and even finding unconventional solutions to everyday problems.
- **Leadership Skills**: Although you haven't held a formal leadership role, you may already have qualities that make you an exceptional leader. These include things like: the ability to take initiative and the ability to lead and motivate others. Building

these qualities can really set you apart when you enter into the job market.

- ○ **Organizational Skills**: Are you more organized than most? Are you efficient with setting priorities and managing your time? Not only will these skills help you with your goals, but if you start obtaining certificates now, you can translate this into the real world when you are applying for jobs.
- ○ **Technology Literacy**: If you are proficient in software programs, social media management, or digital communication, technology literacy can open doors through trade certificates or pursuing a four-year degree.
- ○ **Financial Literacy**: If you are naturally good with numbers, consider seeking out certificate programs that can put you to work right away.
- ○ **Networking**: Building successful relationships is a skill. If you are good with this, how can you use this skill right now to help further your goals or career?

Remember, your skillset is not limited to these examples. You may have a unique combination of talents that sets you apart. Embrace your individuality and explore how your skills can be transferred and adapted to different opportunities and roles.

As you move forward on this journey to emancipation, consider how these skills can be utilized now. Will your organizational skills help you thrive in college? Can your problem-solving abilities contribute to entrepreneurial endeavors? Take a moment to reflect on how your talents can be harnessed to create meaningful outcomes in your life.

By tapping into your current skill set, you position yourself for success right now. Embrace that power that lives within you and allow it to lead you.

Anticipating Challenges: Preparing for the Defensive Line

In football, we spend countless hours studying our opponent. We do this by watching their footage and analyzing some of their strategies. This is a great way to prepare for the unexpected. I want you to get in the habit of doing the same thing with your dreams and goals. While you are making your plans for your future, take time to consider the things that could go wrong in the process. By proactively preparing for the defensive line, you can navigate the challenges effortlessly.

Truthfully, life is full of unexpected twists and turns. As you move towards your emancipation, it is important to acknowledge that there will be obstacles and setbacks along the way. Accepting that is going to give you the competitive edge that you will need to keep fighting back anyway.

Below are some tips that have helped me along the way in preparing for the unexpected. As you are reading each one, take some time to really analyze it. Are you using that tool to your full advantage already? If you are not, what are some ways that you can get the most out of the tools available to you?

- **Knowledge is Power:** During your time in the system, you will be greeted with a lot of flyers and information. Read all of it. You never know what webinar or free event can seriously help you. The more you know, the more information you will have when you are making decisions for your future.
- **Build a Support Network**: No one ever wins alone. You need a great team and support system around you. You deserve a mentor and friends who will keep you accountable. If you don't already have these things, now is the time to go in search of them. Seek out individuals who have navigated similar challenges and can offer you valuable insights and advice.
- **Develop Resilience:** Long story short, you have to develop an ability to bounce back from anything. Life doesn't get easier - you just get stronger. Getting stronger in this area is not something

that you can do by accident. Set yourself up for success by developing and using coping strategies that help you. Also, develop a plan to help you stay committed to your goals even when life throws you for an unexpected loop.

- **Plan for the Future:** So far, we have spent this entire chapter talking about the importance of developing a plan. That's because having a plan is how you give yourself something to look forward to. Trust me, I know how easy it is to fall into a space of depression or sadness, and I can personally tell you that having a plan helped me to avoid some of those dreadful places. If something happens to you that throws your plan off of your original course, that's OK. Take a moment to join in a huddle with your support network and your case worker and formulate a new one. Whatever you do, just make sure that you always have something to be working towards.

- **Embrace Flexibility:** Again, life doesn't always go as planned. Make sure that your plan includes a little wiggle room to be flexible. Have a plan in place for how you maneuver through those times.

- **Prioritize Self-Care and Your Mental Health:** You have to prioritize your physical, mental, spiritual, and emotional well-being. Find ways to rejuvenate yourself. Seek out activities that help you foster a healthy mindset and seek support when you need it. This season of life can and will be challenging, but I have faith that you can and will succeed. Make sure you show yourself some extra love, but recognize that rest is productive when you are doing what you are supposed to do.

The Facts

In this chapter, we talked about the importance of setting goals and coming up with plans to help you achieve them. This chapter was so important for me because this one was the hardest to learn and apply in the real world.

I still remember a time when I believed I had a foolproof plan. Thanks to my football achievements, I knew I was going to be able to secure scholarships and play football somewhere, and I did just that. I received offer letters and scholarships from some of the best colleges in the nation. However, my lack of self-advocacy and awareness led to a major setback. Sadly, I fell short of meeting the foreign language requirement necessary for admission, and suddenly, I needed a brand new plan. With only three years until my emancipation date, I knew I had to do something fast to make sure that I didn't end up homeless and alone.

We'll get into the rest of that story later, but for now, I want you to take a moment to consider some things that you learned in this chapter. How will you implement those tools that I've given you to make this period of time easier for yourself? Then, I want you to use your journal to complete the activity for this section.

2

Lesson 2: Use Short-Term Goals to Help with Your Plan

Just like a football game is composed of individual plays that contribute to a final score, your journey to emancipation is made up of countless moments, thoughts, and decisions that can push you toward success. In this chapter, we will explore the power of short-term goals and the transformative mindset needed to make the most of your time in your program.

Trust me, short-term goals play a super important role in your transitional period. They act as a guide towards your bigger picture. They help you navigate all of the challenges and opportunities that will arise. By focusing on short-term objectives, you can maintain a sense of control and progress that will help you on your way to long-term success.

But it is not just about setting any goals. In order to maximize your potential, we'll dive into the art of creating SMART goals. These goals are Specific, Measurable, Achievable, Relevant and Time-bound. By creating goals that fit this kind of criteria, you will make sure that you are always working towards something that is realistic, trackable, and inalienable with your long-term goals.

Throughout this chapter, we will also explore the importance of developing a winning mindset. This mindset recognizes that the program is a temporary phase in your life. By accepting this reality and perspective, you can get serious about strengthening your resilience and adaptability.

Remember, the journey toward your dream is not short or straight. It is a dynamic game that is going to require you to constantly analyze, self-reflect, and adjust when necessary.

Now, get ready to step on the field of short-term goals, where each accomplishment acts as fuel to your momentum to propel you to the end zone of success. Lace up your mental cleats and prepare to seize the clock because, in this chapter, I'll equip you with the tools you need to unleash the short-term triumphs in the game of transition.

> " REMEMBER, THE JOURNEY TOWARD YOUR DREAM IS NOT "
> SHORT OR STRAIGHT. IT IS A DYNAMIC GAME THAT IS GOING TO
> REQUIRE YOU TO CONSTANTLY ANALYZE, SELF-REFLECT, AND
> ADJUST WHEN NECESSARY.

The Power of Smart Goals

Before we dive deep into the world of short-term goals, let's take a minute to understand why they are so important. On the field, in a real game, quarterbacks usually know which play is happening next. However, every now and then, a team that you've studied will pull out a play that you weren't expecting. Being able to analyze the situation and focus on that next step allows a quarterback to adjust the play if they need to. This key has helped me pivot so many important moments of my own life. That is why I'm spending so much time talking about goals and the importance of them. I want you to realize that they are an essential part of success.

In a real game, if you are able to successfully move the ball ten yards, then you have another opportunity to push toward that end zone. I want you to see your short-term goals the same way. Every time you check something off, you are one step closer to your bigger picture - even if it is going to take you some time to accomplish. Those small victories will continue to push you in those moments when life gets hard.

In the introduction to this chapter, I introduced you to SMART goals. Let's break that down even further.

Specific

When you are planning out your goals, please be sure to be as specific as possible. Instead of saying something like, "I want to go to college," decide on the school and program that you want to get into. This allows you to have some clear direction on what you are working towards. This is important because each school and program may have its own requirements. Being specific allows you to keep those requirements in mind when you are setting your short-term goals.

Measurable

I love including something that I can measure in my goals because it allows me to track my progress. Maybe you want to bring your grades up this semester. Instead of just saying that you want to earn better grades this semester, you can create a short-term goal that is measurable and can put you on track to accomplish that. For example, you can say, "I want to study one hour a day - three days a week." Having a specific goal will allow you to have something to work towards - even on those days when you don't feel like it.

Achievable

It is incredibly important that you are not creating more stress than you need to for yourself. While you do have more pressure than most of your peers, that does not mean that you should set goals so big that you don't have the energy or the hope to achieve them. Instead, write out goals that are realistic to your present situation and what you can realistically handle. Each goal should be a challenge, but it shouldn't leave you feeling defeated before you even start.

Relevant

Make sure that your short-term goals align with your long-term vision. When you are setting your short-term goals, make sure to take some time to ask yourself, "How does this goal bring me closer to my desired outcome?"

Time-Bound

When setting your goals, it makes it more beneficial when you attach a deadline. Doing this will create a sense of urgency and help you track your progress.

Now that I've explained SMART goals and the importance of aligning them with your long-term goal let's work through a couple of examples together.

Example: Mark's SMART Decision

Let's imagine that Mark has two years left in high school. To help with his emancipation process, he plans to attend college. Mark wants to use his natural gift of communication to land him a job in marketing. He knows that his struggles with math could severely impact his eligibility for future scholarships. To hold himself accountable, Mark decided to create a SMART goal.

"I will improve my math skills and maintain a minimum grade of a B in all math courses," Mark declares.

This one courageous act empowers Mark to change his approach to math courses moving forward. His goal is **specific,** focusing on improving **his math skills and maintaining a minimum grade of a B**. He knows that achieving his goal is crucial for his eligibility for scholarships.

Furthermore, Mark's goal is achievable. He plans to attend tutoring or math clinics and reach out to his math teacher whenever necessary. He also plans to stay up-to-date with other available resources that could help him enhance his understanding.

Mark's goal is **relevant** because he knows that he needs to have good grades to qualify for certain scholarships. He is keeping the bigger picture in perspective with each decision he makes towards this short-term goal.

Setting a **time-bound** aspect to his goal, Mark commits to maintaining a B grade for the next **two years**, aligning his efforts with a clear timeline.

As Mark progresses through his school years, he continues to self-analyze his commitment to his plan and his performance in his classes. Then, he makes adjustments to his methods when it is necessary. Mark's support system consists of his math teacher, study groups, and one of his classmates to help enhance his learning experience.

At the end of his high school career, Mark was grateful for his dedication to his SMART goal. Not only did it prepare him for his college career, but it also helped him boost his confidence.

Example: Emily's Commitment

Emily is a young woman with ADHD who is determined to manage her condition effectively to achieve her goals. Emily recognizes the importance of setting a SMART goal to keep her accountable and maintain consistency in her treatment plan.

"I will consistently follow my ADHD treatment plan for the next six months to improve focus, enhance time management skills, and reduce distractions, ultimately improving my academic performance and overall well-being," Emily declares.

Committing to her treatment plan is essential in helping Emily succeed in every area of her life. By building habits that include things that help her mental health will make life easier for her. Her goal is specific and straight to the point. She wants to **follow her ADHD treatment plan**. She is able to measure her success by taking her medication every day and following the strategies that she learned in therapy.

Emily's goal is achievable because she is able to attend therapy sessions regularly and take her prescribed medication. She is also able to use planners and time-blocking techniques.

Emily's goal is incredibly relevant as managing her ADHD means that she will enhance her focus, time-management skills, academic performance, and she will positively impact her overall well-being.

By declaring that she wants to follow this for **six months**, Emily has ensured that her SMART goal is something that can help lead her to bigger and better things.

Even though some days were harder than others, Emily managed to stay dedicated to her SMART goals. Six months later, Emily felt more empowered than ever before. She notes improvements in her ability to focus and manage her time. She also is more confident in her ability to manage her ADHD and the impacts it has on her daily life.

Developing a Winning Mindset: The Muscle of Success

In life, you are going to be presented with many options. Some choices will be in your best interest, and others may hinder your long-term goals. That is why I need you to learn to develop a winning mindset.

A winning mindset is the foundation to success because some days are going to be harder than others to show up as your best self; however, if you train this muscle now, you will have it when you need it most. Trust me, there are going to be days when you need the warrior to rise up in you because you are too tired, afraid, or ashamed, so let's prepare now.

A winning mindset includes a set of beliefs, attitudes, and mental strategies that you will use to navigate life with a higher level of confidence, resilience, and determination. This new belief system will help hold you accountable on the days when you feel like quitting.

Now that we know what a winning mindset is and why it is important, let's find out how to develop one for yourself.

A Positive Mindset & Grateful Heart

A winning mindset is fueled with positivity and gratitude. Those two things combined will allow you to see your situation from a completely new perspective. I'm sure if you had it your way, you would have dealt yourself a different hand, but having a winning mindset says that you will win with whatever cards you have in your hand. When you make the decision to see your current situation as a tool needed to propel you to greatness, you start to see your challenges in a different way. What about your present situation can you look at in a more positive or grateful way?

Resilience & Perseverance

A winning mindset thrives on resilience and perseverance. You need the ability to "bounce back" after setbacks because, in life, they are guaranteed to happen. In life, I need you to remember that nothing is permanent. If you are in your winning season - great. Savor it while you are in it because it won't last forever. If you are in a season of despair, great. That means you are in the perfect position to be blessed and receive more than you could have ever imagined. Learn to stay grounded where you are so you never let success or defeat get to your heart.

Growth Mindset

A growth mindset requires you to embrace the idea that intelligence and skills can be developed through dedication, continuous learning, and hard work. Those who have a growth mindset see challenges as opportunities to use the tools that they've been developing.

Goal-Oriented Focus

A winning mindset is goal-oriented. It requires you to have self-discipline while you take time to set clear, specific, and meaningful goals to provide direction and purpose. Those who are committed to maintaining a winning mindset know that they need goals to get them where they want to go.

Belief in Something Bigger Than Yourself

I realize it may be hard to see right now, but I can promise you one thing. Your life has a purpose that is greater than your current situation. The things you are presently living through are molding the resilience and character traits you will need to sustain you on your journey. **Greater is coming later;** you just have to always have the faith to keep waiting for it, and to keep working for it while you wait.

Adaptability

A winning mindset embraces change. It's open to new ideas and opportunities for growth and self-development. You cannot step into the uncertainty of your dreams until you are ready to let go of your desire for control.

The Facts

A winning mindset coupled with SMART goals is the perfect pair. Together, those two things will lay the solid foundation you will need to build anything you want out of life.

Don't believe me? Try it for yourself. Using your journal, I want you to follow the activity for this chapter and create your own smart goal.

3

Lesson Three: Lock In

Are you tired of feeling like you're just surviving? Do you want a deeper sense of purpose, direction, and drive? If so, then I really want you to tune in and learn about the power of focus and locking into your goals.

In this chapter, we will *focus* on equipping you with tools, strategies, and mindset adjustments that are needed to break free from the day-to-day survival mode you've been living in. Instead, let's tap into the limitless possibilities of all of the opportunities ahead of you.

When I talk about focus, I'm not talking about avoiding distractions or concentrating on a task. That's too easy. When I'm talking about focus, I mean a laser-sharp eye view of your next step. I want you to be so locked in that all of your energy, talents, and aspirations naturally gravitate to helping you achieve your goals. That is what I mean when I speak about being focused.

Too often, we find ourselves caught up in all of life's demands, so we lose sight of everything in front of us. I want you to stop doing that. It's not helpful, and you slow down all of your progress.

Together, we will explore the art of focus and the impact it will have on your life as you move forward. We will uncover some simple steps you can use to help cultivate this skill. From setting clear intentions and eliminating distractions to maintaining momentum, I want to equip you with the tools you need to tap into your full potential.

Get ready to lock in and discover the art of mastering focus. It's time to transcend survival mode and step into a different way of living.

> " Too often, we find ourselves caught up in all of life's " demands, so we lose sight of everything in front of us. I want you to stop doing that. It's not helpful, and you slow down all of your progress.

Understanding Survival Mode and How to Break Free

Survival mode is a state of being where you find yourself only able to focus on what needs to be done that day to survive. This means that you do things without a clear sense of purpose or direction. When you are running in survival mode, keeping up with your hygiene might be a difficult thing to do. You may only have the energy to complete one big thing for that day. While it can be a necessary response in a time of crisis, you cannot stay there. Remaining in survival mode can have a negative reaction to your life and well-being.

To break free from living in survival mode it is going to require you to adapt to a different perspective and way of living. Below, I've listed four small changes that you can begin to help you break free from survival mode.

Shift from a Scarcity Mindset to an Abundant One

When we operate in survival mode, it will always look like we don't have enough. We will tell ourselves that we don't have enough time or energy. We may say that we don't have enough access to resources or help, and that mindset will oftentimes hold us back.

That's why I want you to say out loud, **"I have everything that I need right now."** Then, I want you to believe with your entire heart that the statement you just declared is true.

Regardless of what your present situation looks like, you can win with the cards that you have in your hands. You just have to believe that no matter what.

In those moments when things look hard, and you want to revert back to a mindset of lack, I want you to choose one of the following bullet points and decide that you will ignore all of the other lies that your brain wants to feed you about your situation. Instead, I want you to meditate and focus on one of the following declarations:

- I deserve all of the good things that are coming into my life, and I am open to receiving them with a grateful heart.
- I am grateful for everything that I have. I am capable and worthy of receiving abundance and success.
- I release fear and lack, and I embrace everything that surrounds me. I attract opportunities, mentors, and wealth effortlessly.
- I embrace the abundance that surrounds me. I am a magnet for success.
- I am worthy of great things.
- I am capable of being my own advocate. My voice matters, so those around me want to hear what I have to say.
- I am worthy of love, support, and success.
- My dreams matter, and all of my hard work is going to pay off.
- I am the author of my story, and I will choose to focus only on my resilience and strengths.
- I am positively changing my life and those around me by showing up as my best self each and every day.
- I will face all challenges with a positive attitude because I am in control of how I respond to life and those around me.
- I am a valuable member of my community. My present situation does not dictate my worth.

- **I am surrounded by love and support from those who are around me.**

I suggest that you declare these statements whenever you begin to doubt yourself or your situation. I find that they are most effective when you respond to those negative thoughts by replacing them with one of these. Practice these daily to reprogram your mind and shift from scarcity to abundance. Embrace the mindset that abundance is your birthright, and you will open yourself up to limitless possibilities.

Moving from Reactivity to Proactivity

Survival mode will keep you in a reactive state. That means that you are constantly responding to external problems and circumstances. To master focus, I need you to start playing on the offense. Life doesn't *just* happen to you. At any moment, you can choose to play from a different position.

This is why I encourage you to take the time to create goals and make plans. Doing these proactive steps will help you view life from a different perspective. When you are busy making plans or working towards them, you don't have a lot of time to focus on the curve balls that life will throw at you to get you to pivot.

Playing from the offense instead of on the defense is how you regain control of your situation and empower yourself to focus on what is really important.

> LIFE DOESN'T *JUST* HAPPEN TO YOU. AT ANY MOMENT, YOU CAN CHOOSE TO PLAY FROM A DIFFERENT POSITION.

Transition from Fear to a Sound Mind

Survival mode survives off of fear. We can be so focused on the fear of failure, judgment, or just having fear of the unknown. To break free from that, we must embrace a mindset that is not powered by fear.

A sound mind is one that is empowered and focused on something bigger than itself. Having a sound mind means that you are not moved every time a problem arises. No. Instead, you are level-headed and will refer back to your plan or your support system for guidance.

To help with a transition from fear to a sound mind, here are some strategies that I've personally used. They include:

- **Challenge Negative Thoughts**: You have to take note when a thought pops up that is rooted in fear. You do not have to entertain those thoughts. In fact, I want you to stand up for yourself and your future when negative thoughts arise. When a thought pops up that is the opposite of what you are working towards, take some time to declare something else over you and your situation. Don't be afraid to use some of the ones that I listed above.
- **Practice Self-Compassion:** You have to learn to be as kind and gentle with yourself as you are to others. Remember, perfection is never expected of you - only progression. Making mistakes is a part of the process, so change how you look at what others would consider failure.
- **Visualize Success**: Take a few moments a day to see yourself overcoming your challenges and setbacks. You can do this through meditation or even taking the time to write a story of you living out your dreams.
- **Celebrate Your Accomplishments:** No matter the size of your win, you should always be comfortable celebrating yourself.

Shift from Short-Term to Long-Term Vision

We have spent a significant amount of time talking about short-term goals. That is because they are really good at keeping you focused. However, I want you to start challenging yourself to always keep your long-term vision in mind. By using the strategy of visualization and SMART goals, you should always keep your long-term goal as your primary focus. By doing this, you create a sense of purpose and direction that will guide every decision you make. Doing this will help you keep focus on what truly matters.

Eliminating Distractions

To master focus, it is imperative that you eliminate distractions that can hinder your ability to lock into your goals and plans. In this section, I want to explore some common distractions and provide some strategies on how to minimize their impact on your focus.

In order to minimize your distractions, I need you first to recognize what they are. **External distractions** are things outside of you that divert your attention away from the task at hand. These can include things like social media, noisy environments, unhealthy friendships/relationships, and even clutter. While they seem small, these external distractions can pose a big problem over time.

Internal distractions are distractions that arise from within. These include things like negative self-talk, self-doubt, and a lack of self-love and motivation. When we allow ourselves to fall victim to these internal distractions, we can find ourselves engaged in self-criticism, which will cause us to spend more time giving excuses on why things can't be done instead of actually doing them.

When you understand distractions, what they are, and how they hinder you, you can take the offense and put a strategy in place to help you succeed. Through this self-awareness, you take a monumental step to reduce your distractions, and this will empower you to concentrate, engage in tasks fully, and achieve your goals.

Here is a list of some common distractions and some strategies to overcome them. Can you think of anything that I forgot?

- **Cluttered Environment:** Working in an environment that is dirty or cluttered can cause you to keep your mind off of the task at hand. Before you sit down to do your work, I suggest that you organize and declutter your space. This will help eliminate visual distractions that can become potential distractions as you work.

- **Multitasking**: We all like to believe that we are masters of multi-tasking. Well, I'm here to tell you that you are not. Multitasking is simply spreading yourself thin while you bounce from one thing to the next. Imagine how much more productive you could be if you would allow yourself the opportunity to fully engage in one task before you move on to the next one. To help you with this, try prioritizing what needs to be done first. Then, you work in that order.

- **Procrastination:** I have ADHD, so sometimes, it is hard for me to complete a task without an important deadline looming. I used to think that my ability to perform at the last minute was a superpower. Then, I became successful, and it became a hindrance. Now, to help myself, I create my own deadlines. If a teacher says that an assignment is due on the 15th, then I mark on my calendar that it is due on the 10th. This will help me create the urgency I need to accomplish the task without stressing myself out by waiting until the last minute. You can also try breaking tasks down into smaller things that you can accomplish over time.

- **Digital distractions:** Minimize the amount of time that you allow your electronics to distract you. Consider setting some screen time limits. Delete social media apps that take up too much of your time. Use your phone's 'focus features' to help you limit the amount of notifications you receive while studying. Right now, this can all sound like a lot, but if you want it bad enough, then you know there are things you can be doing right now to help yourself.

- **Unhealthy Relationships/Friendships:** Sometimes, when we are in vulnerable situations, it is easy to attach ourselves to people just because it is easier to have someone around than to do life alone; however, as we will discuss in another chapter, not all company is good company. In fact, some relationships have the power and potential to completely derail you from your vision. As you learn to lock in, make sure that you take some time to take inventory of the people that you allow to give you advice and hang around you during your most vulnerable times.

- **Entertaining Negative Thoughts:** Have you ever talked yourself into a bad mood? That's because it is possible to go down a rabbit hole of negativity and get stuck there. If you ever find yourself struggling to get out of those negative spaces, I want to challenge you to speak up to an adult that you trust or your school counselor to find some coping tips to help you further.

- **Perfectionism:** I bet you didn't expect to see this here, but striving to have everything 'perfect' is a great way to put yourself in a distracted state. Some of us can spend so much time obsessing over the little details, that we can end up missing deadlines or creating excuses to push things back further than they need to be. If you know that this is something that you suffer from, I want you to know that mistakes are a part of life. No one around you should ever require perfection from you. Instead, you should always focus on making fewer mistakes than you've made in the past and being committed to not repeating any that you've already learned from. In those moments when you are contemplating the idea of creating an excuse in the name of perfectionism, I challenge you to say the following sentence. **Done is better than perfect.** Then, do the best you can to complete the task in front of you.

- **Overcommitting Yourself:** Have you ever struggled to tell a friend 'no' to something that you didn't want to do? Well, I want you to know that when you promise your time to others, that limits the amount of time that you have to work on your goals. Moving forward, I want you to accept this fact. **No is a complete sentence all by itself**. You are not required to give an explanation for why you said no or feel bad for saying it to someone. Do not allow yourself to become worn down or distracted by concerning yourself with things that hurt you more than they help you.

By identifying and addressing distractions, you can create an environment that supports your productivity, focus, and learning. Minimize external distractions so you can spend your attention focusing on the stuff that matters. Also, don't allow yourself to be your biggest enemy. Recognize that negative self-talk and self-doubt are distractions that are there to stop you from achieving your goals. Then, I want you to use a strategy (or create one) to help you be successful.

> TO MASTER FOCUS, IT IS IMPERATIVE THAT YOU ELIMINATE DISTRACTIONS THAT CAN HINDER YOUR ABILITY TO LOCK INTO YOUR GOALS AND PLANS.

Setting Clear Intentions & Identifying Your Purpose

Setting clear and concise intentions is a powerful practice that can help you lock in and put your energy where it belongs. Before we wrap up this chapter, I just want to stress the importance of setting these kinds of intentions.

By definition, an **intention** is just an aim or a plan. Up until now, we have spent a lot of time talking about the importance of setting plans; however, I truly believe that the reason behind your aim is just as important as the steps you take to help you achieve the goal. When you take a moment to define your intentions, you allow yourself to remain open to finding out your purpose.

Understanding your purpose is an essential part of setting clear intentions. When you know and understand the reason why you do things, it helps to keep you more focused and motivated to complete the task at hand.

To help you with identifying your purpose or the reason why you are doing something, I suggest spending some quality time journaling and self-reflecting. Take a moment to ask yourself some hard questions so you can find the answers you need to define your intentions and clearly explain your purpose. Below, I've listed a few journal prompt examples to help you.

To get the best experience from this exercise, I want to encourage you to be as honest with yourself in your writing as possible. Take a moment to truly express yourself. Remember, you are not turning this in, and no one is going to judge you.

- What career would I pursue if I didn't have to worry about money, and why?
- In my ideal future, I see myself doing...
- A problem that I've noticed in the world that needs to be fixed is.....
- Take a moment to research careers that you would be interested in but seem too hard to accomplish. Then, take a moment to research the action steps required. Once you are completed with that, take some time to reflect on if you would truly want to pursue a career in that field.
- Take a moment to write out a dream you one day want to accomplish that seems scary to you at this stage of your life. Why do you think you are afraid to reach that level of success?
- Take a moment to write down how your journey can help someone else. Is there a career path that will allow you to do that while getting paid?
- What do you genuinely want to achieve in this lifetime? How can you align your goals with your dreams?

- What do you want to be known for?

> " SETTING CLEAR AND CONCISE INTENTIONS IS A POWERFUL "
> PRACTICE THAT CAN HELP YOU LOCK IN AND PUT YOUR
> ENERGY WHERE IT BELONGS.

Write Down the Vision

I was told at a very young age that there is power in writing down the vision you have for your life. From my own personal experience, I've learned that it makes it a lot easier for people to help you when they know the plans that you are working towards. As we wrap up this chapter, I want you to spend some time thinking about your goals, purpose, and intention. Then, I want you to write it out. Because this is your own personal assignment, do it however feels natural to you. If you would prefer to write it as a coach would write out plays, then write it out like that. If you are an exceptional writer, use this time to write out a story of your ideal situation. Once you have that, I want you to challenge yourself by then sharing that with an adult you trust. Maybe it's a foster parent, your case worker, or even a teacher. Regardless, I want you to share that with someone who can help hold you accountable for the vision you have for your life.

The Facts

By using these strategies, I seriously believe that you can alter your life and way of thinking. These things will help you break free from survival mode and develop a mindset that propels you towards your goals. Remember, focus is not just about concentration. It's about aligning your thoughts, actions, and energy with your goals.

You have within you the power to create a life better than the one you are presently living - all you have to do is lock in and stay on course. You've got this.

Now, complete the journal activity for this chapter.

4

Lesson Four: Use Your Gifts & Talents to Your Advantage

Believe it or not, you have, within you, the power to start making money from a natural gift or talent. In chapter one, I challenged you to find creative ways to explore your natural gifts and talents, and in this one, I want to hone in more on that.

When I originally planned out this chapter, I thought it was going to be filled with a lot of information; then, I remembered that I had given you quite a few examples on this topic already. That's when I decided that I would let you do the work this time around.

I want you to take all of the information you've learned up to this point, and we are going to work together to find a gift or talent that you can level into a trade to help you get ahead.

Believe it or not, every day, young leaders like yourself are finding ways to leave their mark no matter what circumstances they have in front of them. I truly believe that you can do the same. You don't have to wait until you graduate college (if that is a part of your plan) to be successful. You can take one of your natural God-given abilities and use them right now to benefit yourself and others, so let's dive deeper into that.

" EVERY DAY, YOUNG LEADERS LIKE YOURSELF ARE FINDING "
WAYS TO LEAVE THEIR MARK NO MATTER WHAT CIRCUM-
STANCES THEY HAVE IN FRONT OF THEM. I TRULY BELIEVE
THAT YOU CAN DO THE SAME.

Who are you?

Now, head over to the activity in your journal for this chapter because I'm going to ask you a series of questions about you and your personality, and I want you to be honest. These questions will help you identify who you are at your core. Knowing these things can help you identify some hidden abilities that you may have within yourself that can help propel you further. This exercise can also help you identify those areas that may hinder you if you do not properly plan for them on your journey.

1. Every business or company you know has a mission statement. The purpose of a mission statement is to help an organization and its clients understand why that business exists. I want you to take a moment and ask yourself, "What is my mission statement? What is the real reason I feel like I was placed on this Earth?" Then, once you know that answer, use the space provided to write it out.

2. What are my greatest strengths?

3. What are some bad habits that I have that I need to change? (Remember, it is imperative that you are honest during this exercise. If you know that you have an issue with time management or procrastination, make sure you list them.)

4. What makes me different from my peers, and how can I use those traits more to my benefit?

5. How do I define success?

6. Am I able to accept criticism? Why or why not?

7. What fears do I have that are presently holding me back from going after what I genuinely want in life?

8. Where did I develop those fears, and what tools can I use now so that I can let go of them?

9. How do I handle setbacks and failure?

10. Using your answer to the last question, is there a way that you can change how you view setbacks and failure to help you in the future?

11. If money were no object, what career path would I choose?

12. Do I have a hard time standing up for myself?

13. How do I see myself?

14. What kind of impact do I want to make in this world?

15. Using your answer to the last question, are your current habits in line with the level of impact that you want to leave? If they are, write another habit that will help. If they are not, how can you change it?

16. What type of activities am I passionate about?

17. What industries align with my favorite things to do?

18. Have their been any moments in my life where I felt a strong sense of purpose or drive? (If you answer yes to this question, please take a moment to write down what triggered that response.)

19. How can I combine my passions into a career path that will leave me feeling valued and purposeful?

20. If I could envision my life 20 years from now, what would it look like? What would I be doing with my life?

21. What feedback have I been given by others about my strengths and skills that I can use to help me choose a rewarding career path?

22. What topics or subjects do I enjoy learning about during my free time? How can I translate this into a rewarding career path?

23. What talents and skills do I have that come effortlessly to me that solve a problem for others?

24. What type of work environment best suits me? (For this question, I want you to be honest with yourself. Do you need to work in an office with a set schedule? Do you prefer a more relaxed schedule that allows you to be out of a traditional office? Whatever your ideal situation looks like, write it down in the space below.)

25. What problems or challenges do I find myself consistently wanting to solve?

Self-Reflection

Now, before we go on to the next section, I want you to take a moment to reflect on the answers you just wrote down. Without thinking about all of the steps that you would need to accomplish, I want you to think of a profession that you believe would best suit you based on your passion, goals, and the natural gifts and talents that you possess. Also, I want you to consider how this profession lines up with your definition of success. Write out your answer in your notebook.

Write the Vision and Make it Plain

For this section, I want you to continue to dive deep. Only this time, this section is going to require you to do a little research. Now that you have a better understanding of a career path that you would enjoy pursuing, let's take a moment to research it a little further. Write your answers down in your notebook or journal.

1. What education or training will I need in order to work in my field of choice?

2. What is a typical salary for someone who works in this field?

3. Can I honestly see myself working in that field? Why or why not?

4. What is the current job market like in that field? (For this question, I want you to research the job market.)

5. What is a typical career path for someone who works in this industry?

6. How does this career path align with my definition of success?

7. What is the typical work culture of this kind of job? Does that culture align with the type of work environment I previously said I would work best in?

8. What kind of growth opportunities exist within my chosen career path?

9. What obstacles will I face working in this industry?

10. What kind of skills do I have that will make me stand out from others competing for a job in this market?

Reflection Time

Now that you've done some research on your chosen profession, I want you to think about a role, or a job that you can currently get into that will be able to prepare you for the role you want later. For example, if you know that you want to be a teacher later in life, what jobs can you apply for now that will look good on your future resume? Take a moment to consider them, and then write them in your notebook or journal.

The Facts

First, I want to say that I am proud of you for digging deep through this chapter. I know that it is sometimes challenging to be honest with ourselves; however, you pushed through and got it done. Good for you.

Before we wrap this up, I want to tell you about something that I credit a lot of my success to. In every area of my life, I have a mentor. I do this for many reasons, but my favorite one is because it is a great way to learn the things you need without having to make a ton of mistakes along the way. A mentor is there to guide you and provide wisdom and direction. They are also great at providing insight and constructive criticism to help you excel in your next phase of life.

As we proceed with these next chapters, I want you to start preparing yourself for a mentor. If you mentioned that you have a difficult time receiving criticism, I want you to focus on that. Put yourself in more positions to be criticized. You'll need it if you ever plan to empower someone to help you on your journey.

5

Lesson Five: Get a Mentor

Have you ever heard the expression, "It's not what you know, it's who you know?" As I grow older, I'm learning more and more just how true that is. For this chapter, we are going to talk about the importance of finding a mentor. Then, I want to give you tools on how to maintain that relationship by being a good mentee. All these things will help you develop a crucial relationship that can propel you forward faster.

A **mentor** is someone who advises or trains. More importantly, a mentor is someone who invests their time, knowledge, and resources to help you succeed. Having someone who has already achieved what you are working towards can give you a unique perspective that your peers may not have. Being trained by someone working in your dream field will help you navigate some of the obstacles you'll face more easily. They will bring their wisdom to your hard work, and together, you'll be able to achieve more - faster.

The Importance of Having a Mentor

A mentor-mentee relationship can be a life-long bond that extends way beyond your present situation. This is why I broke this down into two seperate chapters.

A **mentee** is someone who is trained by a mentor. To help you understand the importance of having a mentor, I've listed a few of my favorite reasons why I personally loved having mentors.

1. **Mentors are a positive role model to have during this challenging time.** Your mentor will be someone who has overcome difficult challenges of their own. Whether they can fully relate to what you are going through now or not, they can empower you with advice, support, or tools they have used to overcome something similar.

2. **Mentors are a great way to receive personalized guidance.** It's not a secret that I struggled in school. However, thanks to some great mentors, I was given the opportunity to have special tests done that allowed me to have special accommodations that helped me in the long run. Despite everything that I've ever achieved, I would not have had some of the opportunities that I've had without the personalized assistance of others who had more knowledge than me.

3. **Mentors are a great way to receive the knowledge you need to succeed.** Your mentor may be someone who is well-connected to people who can help you. They may also be privy to scholarships, internships, or jobs that can help you on your journey.

4. **Mentors are great for social and emotional support.** Mentors typically offer a safe space for you to share all of your challenges, fears, hopes, and dreams. They can help motivate you on days when you feel defeated. They can also offer guidance when they see you doing things that may sabotage your future success. Having a mentor can be a powerful tool to help you during this time of your life.

5. **Mentors are a great way to build your network.** I've met a lot of powerful and interesting people through my relationships with my mentors. Having a strong network is a great tool to leverage as you build your resume.

6. **Mentors can help you build your self-esteem.** Mentors are great at exposing you to some of your strengths and things you might overlook about yourself. Having someone around to help you develop those skills and provide you with guidance in areas you need to grow in can help you feel more confident in yourself and your capabilities.

7. **Mentors are great at keeping you accountable and on track.** Mentors will help keep you accountable for the things you said you were going to do. This is because it is important for you to do your part and be a good mentee. We will talk more about that in the next chapter.

8. **Mentors can be a perfect advocate to have on your side.** Mentors will advocate for their mentees. This can be done by directing you on who you can speak with or speaking up for you directly.

When you are in the foster care system, a mentor is not just a guide; they are a lifeline for you. Trust me. I still maintain a great relationship with all of my mentors because I would not be here today without them.

> " WHEN YOU ARE IN THE FOSTER CARE SYSTEM, A MENTOR IS "
> NOT JUST A GUIDE; THEY ARE A LIFELINE FOR YOU.

How to Find a Mentor

You may be thinking that you don't have access to a mentor. However, I want to challenge this thought. Whether you believe it or not, people around you want to see you succeed. They want you to win so much that they will invest their time, knowledge, and resources to help you do it.

For a moment, I want you to consider one of the goals that you are working towards. Is there someone around you that has achieved that goal before? If not, that's ok. This means you need to go in search of that person. Oftentimes, they are closer than you think.

I want you to think of finding a mentor to be like completing a video game quest. Don't overthink this process and disqualify yourself before you've even begun. You may reach a few roadblocks along the way. You may have to deal with a little defeat during the journey. That's OK, too. Instead of looking at a "no" as negative, I want you to change your perspective. Each "no" puts you closer to a yes. You are playing a numbers game, and the faster you weave out those not part of this journey, the faster you will find the ones who are.

To aid you on your quest, I've included eight different ways you can try to connect with a mentor. I highly encourage you to choose one now. You'll need to decide on one method to try before the end of this chapter.

1. **School & Educational Programs:** Your school is a great place to find adults who want to help children succeed. In fact, some schools may have a mentoring program already established. This is definitely a great place to start.
2. **Community Centers & Organizations:** Try exploring your local community and the nonprofits that serve it. You may find an organization exists to help you on your journey.
3. **Online Mentorship Platform:** There are websites available that can help lead you to your next mentorship. I encourage you to work with an adult and try an online resource to see if this is a solution for you.
4. **Internships & Job Shadowing:** Most business owners will gladly allow you the chance to learn in exchange for your help. Don't be afraid to reach out to companies to ask if there is any availability. Remember, you are playing a numbers game.
5. **Networking Events:** Networking events are a great way to meet other like-minded people. This is a great way to find a mentor.

6. **Alumni Associations:** Try reaching out to your school's alumni associations. This is a group of students who graduated from the same college that you are presently attending. You may find someone who can mentor you and would be willing to help you just because you went to the same school.

7. **Volunteer Work:** If all else fails, get involved in your local community. This is a great way to meet other members around you that can lead you in the right direction.

8. **Personal Connections:** I intentionally left this for the end, and that's because I wanted you to push yourself first. However, if you've tried the steps before and nothing worked, I want you to consider asking your network of friends to refer you to one of their connections. They might know someone in your desired field who would be willing to mentor you.

Remember, finding the right mentor takes time and effort. I don't expect you to do this overnight; however, I do expect you to try *something* today.

> WHETHER YOU BELIEVE IT OR NOT, PEOPLE AROUND YOU WANT TO SEE YOU SUCCEED. THEY WANT YOU TO WIN SO MUCH THAT THEY WILL INVEST THEIR TIME, KNOWLEDGE, AND RESOURCES TO HELP YOU DO IT.

The Facts

No one ever accomplishes great things on their own. This is why it is crucial for you to find a mentor who can pour into you and help you accomplish your goals. Mentors are great at keeping you accountable to your goals, and they are great advocates and assets to have on your journey.

Remember, a mentor is going to do a lot for you. In return, you have to do your part. That's why, in the next chapter, we will discuss the ways you can be the best mentee you can, but first, head over to your journal and complete the activity for this chapter.

6

Lesson Six: Be a Good Mentee

Having a mentor is not only about what they can do for you. That is why, in this chapter, I want to provide you with the tools you need to hold up your end of the relationship.

Nothing worth having in life is going to come easy, and you will have to work to make the relationship with your mentor successful. In this chapter, I'll provide you with the tools you need to be a good mentee, and I'll also give you some examples of scripts you can use to approach your potential mentor.

Becoming a successful mentee goes beyond receiving advice—it's about actively engaging, implementing suggestions, receiving feedback, and demonstrating appreciation for the invaluable time and wisdom a mentor invests in you.

> " NOTHING WORTH HAVING IN LIFE IS GOING TO COME EASY, AND "
> YOU WILL HAVE TO WORK TO MAKE THE RELATIONSHIP WITH
> YOUR MENTOR SUCCESSFUL.

Qualities of a Good Mentee

Let's spend some time discussing some qualities of a good mentee.

- **Open-Mindedness**: A good mentee is someone who is open and receptive to advice. Remember, there are multiple ways to arrive at the correct answer, so always be open to exploring new perspectives and insights. Even when you do not agree with the information or advice being presented, it is important to spend some time reflecting on the information or being open to seeing how it could work.

- **Active Listening**: There is a difference between hearing and listening. You can hear what someone says, but an active listener demonstrates respect and a willingness to understand and absorb the guidance offered.

- **Adaptability**: A good mentee is someone who is flexible and able to easily adapt to change. After all, these are key components in developing resilience.

- **Curiosity**: A desire to learn and a curious mindset leads to active participation and engagement in the mentorship process. Make sure that you always show up with a hunger that your mentor can pour into.

- **Accountability**: A good mentee takes ownership of their actions, learns from mistakes, and demonstrates responsibility in their journey.

- **Respect**: Mentors are incredibly busy people. That is why one of the best things you can do is show them that you value their time by respecting it. You do this by showing up on time, completing assignments by their deadlines, and following through with the things that you said you were going to do.

- **Goal-Oriented**: Remember in the earlier chapters when we discussed the importance of setting goals? Show your mentor that you are ready to achieve great things by sharing your short-term and long-term goals with them.

- **Appreciation**: The best way you can show your mentor you appreciate them and the time they share with you is to utilize everything that they give you. Also, never underestimate the power of telling them how you feel, either through your words or a heart-felt letter or email.

Effective Mentees Communicate

Every successful relationship requires open and honest communication. In the previous section, we talked about the importance of active listening. Now, I want to help empower you to be the best active listener that you can be.

Active Listening

Active listening is more than just hearing what is being said. It requires you to *lock in* with the speaker so you can fully comprehend what they are sharing with you. By actively listening to your mentor, you show them that you value their time and expertise, but more importantly, you allow yourself to learn information that can help you be successful in achieving your goals. When actively listening, it is imperative that you:

- **Pay attention**: Focus on what your mentor is sharing with you. One way to do this is by maintaining eye contact with him/her. If you are not in person, then I want you to try taking notes to make sure that you don't miss any important information that they share with you.
- **Clarify and Reflect**: To make sure that you've properly heard your mentor, take a moment to reflect on what they said. Then, to make sure that you heard them correctly, try to rephrase what they just said in your own language. This allows both of you to make sure that you are on the same page.
- **Avoid interruptions**: When your mentor is speaking, do not interrupt them. Instead, save all of your questions until the end. (Unless they instruct you to do otherwise.)

Like any skill, learning to be a good active listener takes a lot of time and patience. To build this skill, try using these techniques when you are speaking with your teachers or friends. This can help you develop this skill quickly.

Open and Consistent Communication

In order for the steps above to be most effective, they must be done on a consistent basis. That means you will have to play a big part in making sure that all communication is open and effective. Here are some tips to help you do that.

- **Follow-Up**: Get in the habit of following up after communication. One thing that I like to do is have everything in writing. I do this by sending a follow-up text or email where I restate our last interaction. This is a great way to make sure that we are always on the same page.
- **Seek Feedback**: Empower your mentor to give you regular feedback. This lets your mentor know that you are committed to growing.
- **Express Your Needs**: I realize that asking for help is not always the easiest thing to do; however, your mentor is someone who is there to help you. Make sure that you utilize them for the resources that they are. Believe it or not, some mentors may become offended if they later find out about a need that you did not communicate with them.
- **Respond in a Timely Fashion**: Your mentor should receive communication from you in a timely fashion. To make the most out of your relationship, do your best not to have your mentor waiting around for your responses.

> " EVERY SUCCESSFUL RELATIONSHIP REQUIRES OPEN AND "
> HONEST COMMUNICATION.

Put it All Together

We have gone over the importance of having a mentor. We also discussed the ways that you can do your part to be a good mentee. Now, this is where you are going to take all of your information and put it together.

Below, I've included a couple of different scripts to help empower you when approaching your potential mentor. Remember, it is important that you show up as your authentic self. I do not recommend that you read these scripts exactly as they are. Instead, use them as a guide to help you feel more comfortable.

Approach Your Future Mentor By Email

Subject: Introducing Myself and Seeking Guidance

Dear [Mentor's Name],

I hope this message finds you well. I recently came across your work in [mention his/her specific field or industry], and I was inspired by your accomplishments, particularly in [mention the specific achievement]. As a [enter your position or role here], I admire your expertise and wisdom in navigating the [industry or field]. I am eager to learn from your experiences and seek your valuable guidance in my pursuit of [specific goals or interests]. Would you be available for a brief discussion or meeting at your convenience?

Best regards,
[Your Name]
[Contact Information]

Approach Your Future Mentor at a Networking Event

"Hello, I'm [Your Name Here]. I've been following your work in [industry/field], and I'm impressed by your achievements, particularly [specific accomplishment]. I'm working towards similar goals and seeking guidance. Would you be open to discussing your experiences or offering any advice?"

In Conclusion

To wrap up this section, I want you to notice that in both scripts, I didn't immediately lead with the idea of them being a mentor. Why? Well, it's simple. Being a mentor is a huge commitment. Oftentimes, mentors already have a lot on their plate. They may be running businesses or taking care of children, so agreeing to mentor someone is a demand on them and their time. To be respectful of their time (and yours), you should *ease* your way into the mentor-mentee relationship. This can start by just asking for a few minutes of their time for advice or guidance. Allow this relationship to form naturally so you don't lock yourself into a mentor-mentee relationship that is going to stress you and the other person out.

If you struggle with forming that bond organically, then I want to challenge you to seek out local mentorship programs. There are organizations and programs that exist where the other party knows that you are seeking a mentor. Do not be afraid to utilize these programs for your benefit.

The Facts

Having a mentor is going to help you in every way possible, so make sure you are prepared to learn, work, and grow. This dynamic may sound like a lot of work, but trust me, as you will see in a future chapter, this will benefit you more than you can truly understand right now.

Now, I want you to take some time to complete the journal activity for this chapter.

7

Lesson Seven: Get Serious About Your Financial Future

I know. The thought of planning for your financial future, along with the complexities of speaking about money, can be something that brings up a lot of stress. That is why I want to tackle it head-on.

When I was in the foster care system in California, they had a program that helped students in the system save. This program would match dollar for dollar the amount that the participants put into his/her account. Because I was so focused on football, I was not able to fully take advantage of that program; however, I see how life-changing those funds were for the students who were able to participate. I watched others use those funds to purchase their first car and finance their very first apartment. I realize that when you first hear about it, it might not sound like a big deal, but trust me, it can be if you work the program.

In this chapter, we are going to talk about money briefly and why you should begin financially planning for your future if you haven't already started. Conversations about money typically intimidate us because we sometimes have a tendency to look at what we don't have instead of what we do have. As we work through this chapter together, I want you to challenge every negative thought that comes to your mind. Whether you believe it or not, I want you to say, "**I have everything that I need at this moment, and more will be added as I need it**."

Money Matters

No matter what your situation is, I'm sure we would all like to have a little extra money to help out. That is why I want you to know that talking about money should not be something that discourages you or causes you to stress. In fact, a lot of successful people spend a great deal of their time talking about money. They discuss bills, budgets, savings and investment accounts, tax balances, life insurance, and so much more. In fact, they even take it a step further and empower their bankers or accountants to help them. That is why I want you to change your view about conversations about money. The more you talk about it - the more you'll learn. Then, you can take all of that knowledge to help empower you on your journey.

Some of you may be thinking, "I'm just a child. I don't have to think or stress about money." This way of thinking is just as dangerous as being nervous about talking about it. We all have something we can do today to help us achieve our goals faster. While I will always tell you that money is not everything, we can not ignore the fact that our society is run by it.

Money Isn't Everything

Before we dive into some ways you can learn about money now, I just want to emphasize a point I made in the previous section. **Money is not everything**. When I was in your position, I do remember having days where I didn't always have what I wanted, but I did always have what I needed. Regardless of what your budget looks like at the moment, I challenge you to find a way to look at your current financial situation with a new perspective. Can you find three things that you are grateful for that doesn't cost you anything to have?

You Can Make a Difference Right Now

Despite your present situation and your age, there are several things that you can do right now to get serious about your finances. I suggest that you speak to your caseworker about your goals and desires. They may be able to provide you with more information about each topic that I want to discuss.

- **Develop a Budget**: Even if you don't have an immediate need right now, I've always been in the habit of knowing just how much I need to sustain myself and my life. There are plenty of free templates available that can teach you how to track your expenses and your cash flow. Whether or not you plan to use it right now is irrelevant. This is a basic skill you will need to sustain yourself when you age out of the system, so you might as well familiarize yourself with it now.
- **Look at Your Options for Opening a Checking or Savings Account**: I realize that every state and bank has different requirements. However, I do not want that to deter you from looking into your options. Take a moment to speak with your caseworker or local banker for more information.
- **Get Curious about Credit**: Although you must be 18 to get a loan or credit card, you can begin learning more about how it works now. Again, speak to your local banker to get more information about how you can gain this pivotal knowledge before you make the mistake that a lot of young adults make. Most of us had to learn the hard way about the importance of credit. Do not make that same mistake when that information is out there for you now.
- **Learn How to Make Your Money Work for You**: Successful people know the importance of making their money work for them. They do this by having retirement accounts and trading accounts. A **retirement account** is a designated account in which you save money for retirement. A **trading account** is an account

where you can buy and sell different financial instruments to help you achieve your goals. You may try to convince yourself that you are too young to worry about these types of accounts, but I want to assure you that you are in the best position to begin to plan for these things now.

- **Build Your Resume**: We will dive more into this in the next chapter; however, there are many ways that you can build your resume to help set you apart from your peers. This one committed decision can be a huge difference-maker for you when you go to negotiate your salary with future employers.
- **Find a Financial Mentor**: I realize we just talked a lot about mentors, but we are not finished yet. In my own life, I have multiple mentors for various things. That is why I highly encourage you to do the same.

Remember, this is not a full list of things you can do to learn more about finances. Our goal with this chapter is to build your confidence in talking about money so that it doesn't stress you out. You should always feel empowered to do what needs to be done regardless of the dollar amount in your pockets or bank account.

Take some time this week to discuss at least one of the topics that I've listed with your caseworker or someone who works in a bank and can provide you with that information. Oftentimes, banks have free resources and tools available to provide you with comprehensive knowledge to help set you up for financial success.

Take it a Step Further

To help you feel more empowered to talk about money, I have some resources available online. Make sure you get an adult's permission. Then, I want you to go to lexxikhanpresents.com/dwayne to download my friend Christian's ebook *The Creative Pace to Wealth*. If you use code: **Trainwrecker** at checkout, the book will be completely free!

The Facts

Money isn't everything, but it does matter. Remember, conversations about money should not intimidate you, embarrass you, or stress you out. Instead, you should use the resources around you to empower you to have a better understanding of how money works so you can take control of your financial future.

Now, take a moment to reflect on this chapter in your journal.

8

Lesson Eight: Build Your Resume Now

Regardless of your path, you have the power to build your resume now. A **resume** is a formal document that shows your future employers what skills you hold and any prior work experience that you have. Entering the workforce with a solid resume will help you stand out amongst other people who will be competing for the same opportunities as you.

I know. You might be thinking that you are too young to worry about a resume, but the truth is they are your ticket to unlocking incredible opportunities for your future. As a young adult, building your resume now allows you to put all of your hard work into a formal document that shows employers and others that you have what it takes.

While the idea of building a resume may sound boring, I want to challenge you to change your perspective. Consider your resume to be your highlight reel. This is how you get to showcase every amazing opportunity that you've done. No matter what your next step is, you will need a powerful resume to stand out when you are applying for scholarships, internships, and your dream job.

Ready to get started on your own resume? Let's begin.

❝ CONSIDER YOUR RESUME TO BE YOUR HIGHLIGHT REEL. THIS IS ❞
HOW YOU GET TO SHOWCASE EVERY AMAZING OPPORTUNITY
THAT YOU'VE DONE. NO MATTER WHAT YOUR NEXT STEP IS,
YOU WILL NEED A POWERFUL RESUME TO STAND OUT WHEN
YOU ARE APPLYING FOR SCHOLARSHIPS, INTERNSHIPS, AND
YOUR DREAM JOB.

The Components of a Resume

Depending on your desired field, your resume may or may not have everything outlined. Keep in mind that your resume may not have all of the fields listed as you are just now starting out.

- **Header with Contact Information**: This is where you will list your name, phone number, address, and email address. If you have a LinkedIn profile, consider adding it to your header.
- **Objective or Summary**: This section allows you to explain to your future employers what your goal is. It also gives you an opportunity to summarize your work history and experience.
- **Work Experience**: Detail your work history, starting with your most recent job or internship. Include the company name, your employment dates, and a description of your roles and achievements.
- **Education**: List your educational qualifications in reverse chronological order, starting with your most recent degree earned or in progress.
- **Skills**: Use this section to highlight your computer, language, or technical skills or certifications.
- **Extracurricular Activities or Volunteer Work**: Use this section to highlight your volunteer work and extracurricular activities. Be sure to share the skills used to perform the work.
- **Awards and Achievements**: Use this section to highlight your success, awards, recognitions, or scholarships.

- **References**: This section is optional; however, you can state that references are available upon request. This lets employers know that they can ask you to provide them the information of people who could vouch for the stuff on your resume.

Remember, you may not have every section when you first start out. That's perfectly normal. Just make sure to actively find ways to build your resume for the future.

Ways To Build Your Resume Right Now

You can begin to build your resume right now. Here are a few things that can help get you started.

- **Do Volunteer Work**: Volunteer work is a great way to gain experience to put on your resume. Not to mention, I know a few people who started off as volunteers and were later promoted to positions because of their work ethic. While this is not always the case, your hard work to help the community never goes unnoticed or unappreciated.
- **Seek Out Job Shadowing or Internships**: Many employers offer summer internships, jobs, or job shadowing opportunities. These are great ways to learn skills to put on your resume while establishing a good reference for you to use in the future.
- **Part-Time Job**: I realize that this won't work for everyone; however, if you can handle it, then working a part-time job is a great way to earn an income while gaining some experience for your resume.
- **Join Clubs or Extracurricular Activities**: Join organizations, programs, clubs, or sports. These activities will show your involvement and dedication beyond academics.

The Facts

Building a resume now will definitely help you in the future. After you've reviewed this chapter, head over to your journal to complete the activity that goes along with it.

9

Lesson Nine: Watch the Company You Keep

With my best friend Jordan

While I could use this time to list out the reasons why it is important to be mindful of the company that you keep, I want to share this. **I would never have accomplished the things I have in life if I didn't surround myself with people who were on a similar mission.**

To this day, I only surround myself with people who have the passion and hunger to outwork me. Why? It's simple. You are not always going to feel your best. That is why you need people to inspire and motivate you, but more importantly, you need those who will keep you accountable. When I made the decision to surround myself with people on a similar mission as the one I was on, my life immediately changed for the better.

As you are in the process of doing an inventory of those in your life, I want to honestly assess all of the relationships you have. That means I want you to take a moment to reflect on the romantic ones you have as well. My hope is that you are too focused and locked in to be worried about your relationship status, but I know how

On signing day with my friend AJ Hotchkins

it goes. It feels nice to have someone around to love on you when the world sometimes feels like a cold and lonely place. Regardless, our romantic relationships have the power to inspire or leave us too drained to continue trying.

The Facts

Bad company will corrupt even the best people. Do not allow yourself to miss out on opportunities to succeed just because you want to look cool today. Be empowered to cut off the friendships that don't serve you or your goals. You and your future deserve it.

Now, I want you to head over to your journal, and complete the activity for this chapter.

10

Lesson Ten: Build a Solid Support System

I know that life is hard when you don't have the safety net that many of your peers have. However, in your unique situation, you still have the ability to surround yourself with the *family* you choose to create.

Over the years, I've learned the importance of surrounding myself with people who want to see me win. Honestly, it took me a little while to remove myself from the "bad crowd" so I could begin to work on my future. Once I learned that lesson, I began to enjoy the journey of seeking out people who wanted to help me with my dreams.

By now, you've learned about mentors and the importance of being selective of your friend group. However, I want to encourage you to delve into the importance of being intentional about building your support system. Your support system can include friends, co-workers, teammates, teachers, counselors, and other individuals who genuinely care about you and your future.

Understanding the Components of a Solid Support System

Your support system includes a variety of people. Your support system can include:

- **Friends**: Real friends will push you to achieve great things. Building healthy friendships can provide you with emotional support and memories to last a lifetime.
- **Mentors**: Mentors can help you in every area of your life. That is why I have many mentors in different fields of my life. I have a mentor for business, career, and finances.
- **Teachers & Coaches**: Educators and Coaches want to see you win. That's why they offer guidance, knowledge, and support.
- **Nonprofit Organizations**: There are organizations that exist to help people in your current situation. Don't be afraid to seek them out and complete an intake. You never know how they can help until you let them know what you need.

Ways to Nurture Your Support System

Building a strong support system will require some work on your part. This is why you need to be intentional about pouring back into those who pour into you.

Communicate: In this day and age, vulnerability is a superpower. Own yours. Share the details with your mentor or counselor. They love it when you keep direct and easy lines of communication.

Give Back to Others What They Give to You: Friendships, mentorships, and relationships are a two-way street. Always be ready to speak life into those who help you succeed.

Use the Information They Provide: Having the education to do better and not use it is just silly. When those around you give you guidance and advice, be sure to use it.

Become the Best Possible Version of Yourself Possible: The best way to show yourself to those in your support system is to rise to the challenge. You have within you the power to overcome every obstacle that ever tries to slow you down. Show it by showing up for yourself consistently.

The Facts

Success is never achieved alone. You will need a team. Now that you've learned more about building and nurturing a solid support system, head over to your journal to complete the activity.

11

Lesson Eleven: Constantly Work to Improve Your Relationship with Your Mentor

I told you there were times when I was going to get repetitive. That is why we are once again talking about the importance of constantly working to improve your relationship with your mentor.

For this chapter, I plan to do it a little differently than I have with the other ones. On the pages that follow, you are going to hear from some of my mentors who have helped me along the way. My mentors will speak to some of the obstacles I had to overcome and how they properly equipped me to handle all of the things that life threw at me. The reason I want to do it this way is because I want you to see the significance of working on the relationship you have with your mentors.

I credit my success to every single teacher, counselor, and mentor who took time out of their busy schedules to pour into me and help me advocate for my future. That is the reason I stress the importance of finding one and then respecting him/her enough to implement the tools they provide to you. As you are reading their stories, I want you to think of any similarities that exist between my story and yours. Then, when you are done, I want you to take a moment to reflect on what you've learned as your journal exercise for this chapter.

A Message from Glae

Life has a funny way of surprising us with unexpected moments of inspiration. There are times when you believe you're meant to inspire others, but as life reveals itself, you realize they were the ones who inspired you all along....

He has experienced challenges and obstacles, both in life and in the foster care system, but his positive mindset has made him a champion at making the necessary changes to his own life by believing in himself!

Dwayne's story invites you to reflect on your life journey. Use his story to find the meaning in your own hardships, but also the joys you experience! Dwayne's story should also serve as a reminder that you are NOT alone, even though it may always feel that way. **Dwayne's story personifies the spirit of what it means to pursue your dreams and, against all odds, to achieve them.**

To everyone who has experienced the foster care system, Dwayne's story will sound familiar. Dwanye's story is an invitation for you to find comfort in the knowledge that you are not alone! He is someone who understands your struggles firsthand. Let his experiences be an inspiration for you to embrace your own unique journey, and may his unwavering commitment to himself ignite a flame of resilience and compassion within you! Be your own champion, believe in yourself, and fight for the life you have always wanted and deserve!

As someone who entered Dwayne's life to serve as a role model and friend, I could never have imagined how these roles would change! Today, I am beyond grateful to be inspired by Dwayne's resilience, strength, and unwavering commitment and belief in himself. He continues to surprise me and make me endlessly proud to call him our son!

"Dwayne's story should also serve as a reminder that you are NOT alone, even though it may always feel that way."

A Message From My Mentor Tammy

I will never forget the first day I met Dwayne. It was at the homecoming rally when this tall, athletic, happy-go-lucky young man walked up to me and, out of the blue, asked me who I was. I told him my name, and he replied, "I'm Dwayne, and I'm in foster care."

Of course, this was not a typical conversation starter, but with that first interaction, we connected immediately. We didn't connect because he was in the foster care system; we connected because Dwayne was unique and instantly had a charisma unmatched by most high school students. He had a never-ending smile that warmed everyone's heart, an inner drive that would not allow him to give up, and, most importantly, a kindness that all those around him would gravitate to. His village was full from the start.

Growing up in the foster care system and attending approximately twenty-five different schools, Dwayne had every reason to give up, but his village recognized he would not. While most students have access to transportation, just getting to school was not easy for him. He did not drive, so he had to take the city bus. Even when he missed the bus, he'd walk three miles to school because missing his classes was not an option.

One day, it was pouring rain, and I saw him walking up the hill to school, soaking wet. I pulled over, he ran to my car, and what did Dwayne do? Simply smiled, said thank you, and went to school wet. This foster care student never missed a day of school.

Dwyane knew school was his only way to make it in life, and he knew he needed a community beyond the foster care system. What was concerning to me was that Dwayne had attended so many schools in his life, so he did not have the academic skills needed to succeed on his own. The first time I saw his writing, I was deeply concerned. Not just because of his skills, but because he lacked the resources to help him as well. At the time, Dwayne did not have a computer. Thankfully, each of Dwayne's teachers would send him to my classroom to use my computer to complete his work. They gave him extended time to complete his work, helped him make the necessary corrections before he submitted his work, and supported him not just through academics, but showed care for his emotional well-being as well. The term "it takes a village" is so very true in Dwayne's situation. His teachers worked with him, encouraged him, held him accountable, and quickly became his village.

During his senior year, Dwayne had to pass the California Exit exam, which he needed to pass to graduate from high school and to be able to go on to college. Thankfully, his football coach, who was also a special education teacher, tested Dwayne and found that he qualified for the support services from the special education program. Because he had moved so often, Dwayne was never in one place long enough for any teacher to see the need to test him. With the extra support, Dwayne passed both of the tests and was ready to graduate with the opportunity to attend our local community college to play football.

Before he moved on from high school, Dwayne was voted the Most Inspirational Student. During our academic rally, Dwayne allowed his story to be told. The standing ovation from the staff and students seemed to go on forever. During the video, it was mentioned that Dwayne could not have a computer while in the foster care system. By the end of the rally, staff and students collected enough money to purchase Dwayne a computer for college. Dwayne asked me to hold on to the money until he was moved into his transitional housing. Once he was settled, we went shopping for his computer. To witness the joy and sense of accomplishment he felt then, is a memory I will never soon forget. His village continued to grow.

I recently was walking with one of the teachers who had an incredible impact on Dwayne. During our walk, my phone rang, and it was Dwayne. I quickly answered it and told him who I was walking with. In the loudest, most excited tone in his voice, he told the teacher hello, that he missed her, and that he would be by soon to see her. I am not sure at that moment who was happier, Dwayne or the teacher. The village worked to get Dwayne across that finish line, and he has never forgotten the school and the teachers who gave him the opportunity to succeed!

Why is Dwayne's story one of success? He had the courage to communicate with his teachers, ask for help, and trust in their guidance. Today, he is one of the only alumni allowed on campus to speak to students, tell his story of resilience, and hopefully make a difference in other students' lives. Dwayne has quickly become our village. We are lucky to have him.

" Why is Dwayne's story one of success? He had the courage to communicate with his teachers, ask for help, and trust in their guidance. "

A Message From My Mentor Gabby

 Dwayne and I met at the start of the spring semester of 2016, when I was assigned as his tutor. He was a spring transfer student, which is difficult for any student as they miss out on all the university orientation programs that those starting in the fall have access to, including the summer bridge program that starts the summer before the fall semester begins. As I will share, this was only one of many barriers Dwayne faced during his time at UC Berkeley. Of all the students I tutored in the four years I worked with Cal student-athletes, Dwayne was by far my favorite (to my other tutees reading this, I appreciated working with you also). I am honored to be able to share a bit about the time Dwayne and I worked together.

First, a bit of background on how I became a tutor for student-athletes at UC Berkeley. I started working at the Cal Athletic Student Center in the spring semester of 2012, which was a semester after I started my Ph.D. in Social and Cultural Studies of Education. I had been a middle school teacher for a few years before going back to grad school. As a teacher, I felt powerless to change the school policies and community conditions that harmed the low-income students (predominantly students of color) in my classroom. I decided to get my Ph.D. so that I could learn more about why my students struggled and what I could do about it. I also felt that having those letters after my name would make it easier for me to be heard in spaces that, as a brown, tattooed, low-income woman, I often wasn't invited to.

When I got to Berkeley, I needed to find work to support myself. I had worked as a tutor before and after working as a teacher. Of all the jobs on campus, tutoring at the Athletic Student Center, where I could work with Black and Brown student-athletes who were struggling at an elite university, seemed like the best fit for my skill set and passions. I tutored at the Athletic Student Center for five years, the last few of which overlapped with another tutoring position I took working for the Berkeley Underground Scholars Initiative with students who had been incarcerated.

I met Dwayne in my 4th year working at the Athletic Student Center. The first two things that stood out to me when I first met Dwayne was how tall he was and how sweet he was. The second two things that stood out to me were how smart/observant he was and how much he struggled with academic work. For example, I found an old email from Feb 22, 2016, where I shared with another tutor how smart/observant he was:

He is awesome to work with once he warms up -e.g., tonight we were talking about intersectionality, and he felt that it was basic common sense and couldn't believe it when I told him that it took black feminists to show white feminists that black women could be oppressed by gender and race. He kept bringing it up even when we started talking about something else.

The most notable area he struggled with was writing. It became clear early on that his difficulties with writing stemmed from both the substandard education he had received before coming to Berkeley, and the number of learning disabilities he had that had never been addressed. UC Berkeley had (maybe still has) a very rigid policy where they would not provide classes to help students catch up to college level i.e., remedial classes, and, at the time, there was no policy in the Athletic Student Center to screen for learning disabilities. Student-athletes needed to keep a C average to be eligible to play, meaning that students who did not get a good education before coming to Berkeley and those who had unaddressed learning differences were up against almost insurmountable barriers to success. Those were the barriers that Dwayne faced when I met him.

Dwayne was very invested in his education, and I was invested in helping him succeed educationally. I advocated for the Athletic Student Center to help students get tested for learning disabilities and then to help them get connected to the Disability Resource Center to get the accommodations the university lawfully had to provide them. By the fall 2016 semester, Dwayne was receiving his accommodations, which was a good start, but those accommodations, per UC Berkeley policy, could not include the writing skills help that Dwayne desperately needed.

Dwayne and I were only slated to work 6 hours/week, but more than once, we would spend 10 hours in a day working on a single paper. We would start with Dwayne talking about what he wanted to say in his paper, which is where he shined. He then would write out what he wanted to say. We would then spend hours developing each sentence and then each paragraph. I don't think I ever told Dwayne this, but when he came to Berkeley, he was writing at about a second-grade or third-grade writing level. I had no idea how we were going to keep his C average, but I was determined to support him in any way I could.

> " Dwayne was very invested in his education, and I was " invested in helping him succeed educationally.

Those who have not been a student-athlete or worked with a student-athlete may not understand how strict the NCAA rules are in regard to tutoring. When working with formerly incarcerated students, I could make writing revisions on their papers; however, writing revisions are prohibited by the NCAA. All I was allowed to do was to tell Dwayne that his sentence or paragraph was not clear, and then he needed to revise it himself. I would spend hours with him going over the basics of elementary school, middle school, and high school writing and sitting with him while he worked to apply what he had just learned to each sentence. All of his hard work paid off, and within two semesters, his writing had improved immensely and continued to improve throughout the rest of his time at Berkeley.

I spent more hours tutoring Dwayne than I did with any other student, and we often talked about things outside of his assignments. One of the things Dwayne shared with me was that he wanted to write a story about his life. On May 2, 2017, he emailed me a short autobiography that he wrote (sent from his iPhone, but I never asked him if he had written it on his phone). As closely as we had worked together, I had no idea about how hard his life had been and how many things he overcame to get to where he was at that moment in time. He knew that my PhD research was on incarcerated adolescents. After reading his story, I asked him if I could interview him. During our discussion, I learned about how instead of getting support for all the hardships in his life he was criminalized. He credited football for keeping him from being criminalized even more and ending up like many of his peers. I am so grateful to him for sharing his experiences and letting me think through some of my research ideas with him. He definitely helped me more than he might realize in figuring out who I am as a researcher.

I am so grateful that I am still connected with Dwayne and look forward to hearing about how his life is going in terms of football and beyond. I cannot understate how proud I am to see this young man, who at one time struggled with writing, writing a book about his life. I know that his story can inspire others to keep moving forward no matter the obstacles. I am sure there is a football metaphor in there somewhere.

-Gabby Medina Falzone

A Message From Coach Kevin

Believe...

It was the Spring of 2012 and we had just come off the worst season in coaching I have ever had. We had a strong group of sophomore athletes coming back with a great group of juniors so the future was bright. We were working on revamping our entire program from top to bottom as we were in the weight room one day when I received a message that we had a new student who was interested in playing football.

As you can imagine, when Dwayne walked up, the possibilities seemed endless as this 15-year-old manchild stood actually towered over me. As a program, we had a mantra to "BELIEVE" and threw Dwayne right into workouts, expecting him to fit right in. Unfortunately, Dwayne wasn't ready, and I believe we created more stress for him than support. Although Dwayne was a big child, we assumed he had to have a football background, and actually told us he had played a little bit. Dwayne was restless as he settled in and started to become upset with some of his teammates because he was not as strong. It was here that we realized we needed to take a step back and listen to where Dwayne was and why he was so quick to argue or fight.

We brought Dwayne into my office one day after weights and learned who he was but, more importantly, where he had come from. As I reflect back, I believe we were the 3rd or 4th high school in 4 semesters he had attended, and it all started to make sense as he continued to talk. Dwayne was a great child who just didn't trust those who were around him because of his constant moves in schools and homes. Our staff determined from our conversation we needed to go slow to help support him and gain his trust, and once we did that, the story of Dwayne Wallace began to come to life.

Dwayne's Coachability & Work Ethic

We just finished our off-season training and were moving into Spring and Summer training. Dwayne was working harder but still not as hard as he could almost as if he was just going to try and get by as a big child. Unfortunately, for Dwayne, we played in one of the toughest high school conferences in the nation and although being big was important you also had to be strong, physically fit, and absolutely resilient to compete in every play. We had him play up with the Varsity early on but his work ethic did not match his ability. He was often last in conditioning and often chose to walk around and instead of competing at a high level. In addition, Dwayne was not processing information as fast as his teammates which was creating a barrier for him and increasing his frustration. One of his new closest friends took Dwayne on and said quit arguing, play next to me and I will get you through every play and support you in getting better. Dwayne began to buy in and his growth started to take off.

Dwayne's Temperament

Although Dwayne had some struggles and frustrations early on as he became more successful in his play and knowledge his demeanor started to change. Dwayne went from the child who was last and often being called out by his teammates to the guy out in front encouraging others to compete. His Junior season  finished up and scholarship offers started coming in for other teammates that Dwayne felt he was just as good as. As we prepared him for the spring recruiting season we had to be honest and make him aware of his transcripts and what it meant. We talked to him about his options moving forward if he wanted to continue in this game and let him know he would have to be a JC transfer guy if he was going to compete at a 4-year school. He was upset with our conversation and said "I can make it now" We said you definitely can but we need to improve your academic skills to get you there. When the 4 year coaches started coming through in March we had Dwayne talk to every one of them so he could better understand his path after high school. Everything started coming together after that point and Dwayne was on fire to compete at the highest level he could. He began to crave the structure of our football program and was working outside of practices with another group to be the best he possibly could.

Dwayne's Ability to Overcome Obstacles

Dwayne faced his fair share of challenges during his journey, but his determination and perseverance always shone through. Whether dealing with injuries or tough losses, he remained resilient, using each experience to fuel his growth. As he finished his Senior football season, Dwyane began networking with anyone he could to help support him in the process. The coaches at the Junior College were in his corner and fighting to set a path for him to have an opportunity in the future. At this point, he had matured into his own advocate, armed with the resources to compete at the highest level he could.

> " Dwayne faced his fair share of challenges during his journey, but his determination and perseverance always shone through. "

It's Been a Blessing...

I have been blessed to coach a lot of great athletes in my 25-year career as a coach. I am excited and even more grateful that I got to be a part of this remarkable story. Dwayne has matured into a caring man who understands the value of hard work and self-belief. He has always been willing to come back and tell his story and pour into high school students the value of self-advocacy. I am so proud of where Dwayne is today and he will always be a proud part of my life. Dwayne Wallace became a champion through athletics and as he transitions into the next chapter of life he is becoming a champion of those he serves.

A Message From My
Program Director David

I love my job as a residential program director, working with at-risk youth. It is my way of giving back as I remember those who supported me through my difficult childhood. I am motivated by the potential I see in these amazing young people and I am so proud of the hurdles they have overcome. Dwayne was one of those incredible youth. I remember him as a humble and respectful teen, who put others first and was always willing to help. He chose to avoid conflict whenever possible, but if one should arise, Dwayne would be the first to offer solutions instead of becoming a part of the problem.

Working with Dwayne was a wonderful experience. He was a young man who was wise beyond his years. He was focused, he had a goal and he surrounded himself with positive influences to help him stay on the right path. Dwayne never hesitated to ask for help in achieving his goals. He was hungry for knowledge, and he often asked for advice on a wide range of topics. Dwayne wanted to be successful, and he immersed himself in his schoolwork and training for football. Dwayne selected friends who had the same drive for study and training as he, recognizing it was the best way to achieve his goals.

Dwayne took advantage of all the resources that were offered in our program, growing his self-confidence to transition into a successful, healthy adult. He learned life skills related to finance, caring for his apartment, shopping, cooking, how to engage with people, coping with stress and many others. He built relationships with staff in our transitional program and his college campus, who continued to support his goals. Dwayne's openness to listen, to learn, to accept recommendations set him apart from most of his peers. Whenever Dwayne experienced any sort of struggle, he sought help from tutors and guidance from individuals whom he trusted and admired.

One of the challenges Dwayne had to overcome was his immigration status. The transitional program manager and I worked with Dwayne toward receiving U.S. residency status, in order to enroll in college. This put him on a path toward a degree and his football career.

Dwayne gives back to the community he came from. On several occasions, he has shared with youth in our program about his experiences, about goal setting and ways to reach their dreams. He continues to check-in with me, letting me know how he is doing, and offering to contribute his time to support at-risk youth.

How did Dwayne reach the goals he set for himself? The bottom line- he was a young man who set goals, he asked for help to achieve them, he used the resources provided, and he never gave up.

" How did Dwayne reach the goals he set for himself? The bottom line- he was a young man who set goals, he asked for help to achieve them, he used the resources provided, and he never gave up.

12

Lesson Twelve: Never Give Up

Life isn't always fair, and I believe that is something that we can all agree on. A lot of us have had to survive some pretty traumatic things to arrive where we are today. I know in my introduction I told you that I planned on giving you more of my story, and I feel like this chapter is a great place to do it.

I was originally born into less-than-ideal circumstances. When I was born in London, my older sister did the best she could to take care of me and her other children. I stayed there until I moved to Jamaica, where I resided with my mother. I'm not sure if it was my ADHD or if it was because I had a hard time with authority, but I was constantly finding myself in the wrong crowds and in trouble. This forced my mom to send me to the United States to live with my father.

Living with him wasn't easy. I was constantly made to feel like an outcast in my own home, and because I've always been my own advocate, he didn't handle the way I spoke up for myself too well. One day, my father purchased brand-new Jordans for all of my other siblings and bought me a cheap pair of sneakers instead. Like always, I decided to tell him just how I felt about being alienated from the rest of the family's joy; however, this time didn't end like the ones before.

Did that call immediately solve my problems? No. Instead, it created new ones where I was forced to bounce from multiple homes and schools. I also had to face the challenges of living in the United States without the legal documentation that I needed. Regardless, I never gave up my fighting spirit, and I continued to tell those around me the things I needed in order to succeed.

My caseworker helped me file my immigration papers, and I continued to fight for myself until I found myself in the right school to help me succeed. Even with all of that, I still had a ton of obstacles ahead of me. I struggled with reading and writing because I had spent my primary years bouncing between different schools and languages. This means that I had to work three times as hard as the rest of my peers just to keep up.

There were days when it felt impossible to continue, but I never gave up. I never allowed those thoughts to defeat me. I walked for miles to school in the pouring rain. I spent countless hours in tutoring sessions. I woke up earlier than some of my teammates so I could study film and learn my plays. I did what was tough because it had to be done.

Were there days when my emotions got the best of me? Absolutely. When I didn't have all of the classes that I needed to go straight to a D1 school, I was angry, and I shed tears as I grieved the missed opportunity in front of me. At that moment, I allowed myself to feel those emotions and understand that I have the power to change the outcome at any time, so I did.

> I'VE ENDURED A LOT OF DISAPPOINTMENT ALONG THE WAY, BUT I NEVER ALLOWED THAT TO DEFEAT ME. I NEED YOU TO DO THE SAME.

Everything that Happens to You Happens For You. It's All for Your Benefit

Before we close out this chapter, I want to share with you guys a few techniques that I've used along the way to help me in those moments when the weight of the world felt too heavy for me to carry.

- **Begin Living and Working By Faith**: **Faith** is a firm belief in what you hope for and an ability to have confidence in something you haven't seen yet. While your brain may try to convince you that you will never achieve certain things because you've never seen or experienced them, I need you to have *faith* that amazing things can and will happen to you if you just keep working through the process. Faith is a beautiful perspective switch; however, if you don't work the plan - it's pointless. Spend some time each day focusing on how much better your situation will get and allow that to fuel you to apply the effort necessary to make that happen.

- **Develop Problem-Solving Skills**: In my friend group, I'm the person they call whenever they need a solution to a problem. That is because years of challenges have empowered me to become really creative in finding alternative solutions. Take some time learning how to identify problems and break them into smaller parts that are easier to work with. Try looking at the issue from all sides and angles. Give your mind some time to get comfortable with seeking solutions instead of allowing it to immediately go into a panic.

- **Nurture Supportive Relationships**: Surround yourself with people who pour into you and want to see you win. Then, make sure you find ways to show those people that you appreciate them. What's the easiest way to do that? Rise to your full potential and go after the life you deserve to have.

- **Face Challenges Head-On**: Life will throw you some curveballs. The easiest way to get through them is to tackle them as soon as they show up to try to interfere with your play. It's really easy to find yourself overwhelmed and stressed if you allow problems to pile up in the background, so to get ahead of the issue, you have to find creative solutions to those challenges as soon as they show up.

- **Learn from Setbacks**: When things don't go according to plan, the best thing you can do is sit back and learn where you went wrong in a situation. In football, we watch film. This allows us to see areas of opportunities for improvement. Part of the reason I encouraged you to begin journaling is because taking time to reflect on your day at the end of each night is a great way to reflect on the decisions you made that day.

- **Let Your Mentors Know When You Are Having a Hard Time**: Your mentor may have additional tips that they can recommend to help you. Sharing those moments when you are struggling is the best way for someone to help you.

- **Develop Coping Strategies**: While training hard is a part of my job, I also consider working out a great strategy to use for your mental health. When life seems too out of control for me, you can find me punching on a punching bag in the gym or training in an open field. In addition, journaling is another great way to cope with stress and anxiety.

- **Practice Self-Care**: You cannot pour from an empty cup. This means that you cannot give what you don't have. Take some time each day to take care of yourself. This can be done by journaling, working out, eating healthy, reading a book that you enjoy, or speaking to a therapist. All of these techniques will help you relax and focus on the bigger picture in front of you.

The Facts

Despite the cards that life has handed you, you have everything within you to become successful. Some of the most powerful people in the world have started off in situations similar to the one you are now. That's how I can confidently say that I know you can do it if you will just put your mind to it.

Believe in yourself and your plan. Then, I want you to use your faith and work to make it happen. You can do it.

13

Lesson Thirteen: Maintain an Attitude of Gratitude

As we prepare to conclude our journey together, I want to share a tip that seems easy in theory but isn't always the easiest task to accomplish.

For me, maintaining an attitude of gratitude has played a significant part in my success. That is because it allows me to focus on the things that can go right instead of the things that are against me.

Leading By Example

One thing I'm grateful for today is this book you currently have in your hand. That's because one day it was an idea that felt like something impossible to do. Now, as a published author, my story gets to count for more than the pain it caused when I was going through everything.

This book would not have been possible without the team of people that helped me get it done. Before I get into all of the people that I want to thank, I wanted to take a moment to give all praises to The Most High because without God none of this would have been possible. I'm thankful for the trials and tribulations that He allowed me to go through because I wouldn't be where I am or who I am today without the challenges that made me stronger.

Laylaa: Thank you for being my motivation not to ever give up. By just existing, you inspire me to be a better man and father. I love you.

Mum: Thank you for the way you raised me. Your countless prayers have always carried me through the years. I love you.

Glae & Rod: I am truly thankful for you guys helping me through the foster care system, college, and now this book. You all have sincerely made a positive impact on my life when I needed it the most. Thank you guys for helping me out throughout my life. You all gave me a safe space to be myself when I needed it most. I appreciate it. Thank you.

Tammy: Thank you for looking out for me and making sure that I made the best decisions for myself and my future. I will never forget you joining me on those recruitment trips and the help your husband provided by training me. Your love and support never go unnoticed. I appreciate you!

Coach Kevin: I want to thank you for accepting me into your football program. You never judged me, and you took the time to learn about my circumstances so you could find the best way to help me succeed. Despite how unpleasant I was to deal with, you never gave up on me, and you saw

through the Hell on Earth that I put everyone else through. Now that I'm reflecting, I was someone who was seriously in need of help and a safe space, and you provided that for me. Thanks, Coach.

Terrell Smith: Thank you for mentoring me in football since high school. You've always motivated me to want to reach the highest level of football, and have been there in my time of need. When I didn't know the next move to make with my career, you were there as a mentor to ensure my football success. I sincerely want to thank you for sharing your connections and wisdom with me. Everyone needs someone there during hard times, and you were there to help me find solutions. You've been that person for me countless times, so again, I'm thankful for all of the memories you've been a part of with me.

Gabby: I would not be where I am today without the countless hours that you helped me! Thank you for everything.

David: Thank you for everything. You've been a great help to me along the way, and I will forever be grateful to you and your sacrifices.

Melinda: Thank you for all of your work in making this book come to life. I appreciate you more than you know.

Keaidy: Thank you for helping me with my dream of being an author. I appreciate you and all of your hard work along the way.

For everyone else who has helped me along the way, thank you! I could have never accomplished the things I have without you and your support.

To get ready to wrap this all up, remember that your mindset is everything. When you have a grateful mindset, you are able to have a clear, positive perception of life. However, when you have an ungrateful, entitled mindset, you will have a clouded, negative outlook on life. In football, perception plays a crucial role. **Perception** is the ability to see, hear, or become aware of something through your senses. It is also the way we understand or interpret something. When a player is on the field, they have to have optimized perception because they have to make several quick decisions, and they need to make sure they are in the right headspace to make that decision to lead them to success.

When we can interpret our life story with a positive mindset and with an attitude of gratitude, we can see how everything in our lives is connected. We can see how there was a purpose for every part of the journey, and we can clearly see what our next move should be. Don't be the type of person that allows your struggles and trauma to control the rest of your life. Don't let one chapter of your story keep you playing small.

The Facts

There was a quote I recently saw that challenged me. The writer of this quote is unknown, but it said, "Someone once told me the definition of hell: The last day you have on earth, the person you could have become will meet the person you became." This quote is being written in a way that assumes you have fallen short and didn't become the person you were meant to become. But what if you did? What if you went through life making the right choices? What if you lived intentionally? What if you looked at every part of your life with a lens of gratitude? There are so many things we can complain about daily, and if we focus on all the negativity, we will attract more of it. So, I want to challenge you to look at your life with an attitude of gratitude. Find the everyday miracles. You've got this.

Join our mailing list today! With adult permission, head over to
lexxikhanpresents.com/bookclub.
Want more information on when Dwayne is getting ready to release
another book?
Go to **lexxikhanpresents.com/dwayne.**

Printed in the USA
CPSIA information can be obtained
at www.ICGtesting.com
LVHW052107120424
777208LV00020B/533